ng housewives,
erior lovers,
ese years ex-
d craft tapes
boxes are plent
t and easily ob
ody.
designs of vari
es such
rattan

PUB GRUB
COOKBOOK

igloobooks

igloobooks

Published in 2014
by Igloo Books Ltd
Cottage Farm
Sywell
NN6 0BJ
www.igloobooks.com

Food photography and recipe development: PhotoCuisine UK
Front and back cover images © PhotoCuisine UK

GUA006 0714
2 4 6 8 10 9 7 5 3 1
ISBN 978-1-78343-458-9

Printed and manufactured in China

CONTENTS

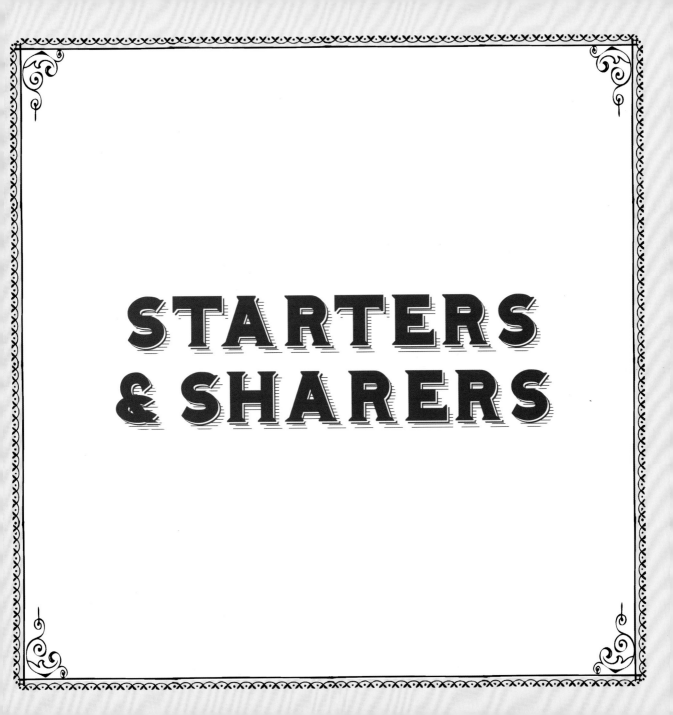

STARTERS & SHARERS

CALAMARI

Serves: 4   Preparation time: 5 minutes   Cooking time: 2 minutes

INGREDIENTS

sunflower oil for deep-frying
200 g / 7 oz / 1 ⅓ cups plain (all-purpose) flour
2 tbsp olive oil
250 ml / 9 fl. oz / 1 cup sparkling water,
    well chilled
300 g / 10 ½ oz / 2 cups squid tubes, sliced
    into rings
tartar sauce to serve
salt and pepper

METHOD

- Heat the sunflower oil in a deep fat fryer, according to the manufacturer's instructions, to a temperature of 180°C / 350F.

- Sieve the flour into a bowl then whisk in the olive oil and water until smoothly combined. Dip the squid rings in the batter and fry for 2 minutes or until golden brown.

- Transfer the calamari to a bowl lined with kitchen paper to blot away any excess oil, then serve immediately with tartar sauce.

TANDOORI CHICKEN WINGS

Serves: 4   Preparation time: 35 minutes   Cooking time: 30 minutes

INGREDIENTS

1 lemon, juiced
3 tbsp tandoori spice mix
8 chicken wings
250 ml / 9 fl. oz / 1 cup natural yoghurt
3 tbsp mint, finely chopped, plus extra to garnish
salt and pepper

METHOD

- Mix the lemon juice with the spice mix and a pinch of salt and rub it all over the chicken. Leave to marinate for 30 minutes.

- Preheat the oven to 200°C (180°C fan) / 400F / gas 6.

- Roast the chicken wings for 30 minutes or until crisp and cooked all the way through.

- While the chicken is cooking, stir the yoghurt and mint together and season with salt and pepper.

- Serve the chicken wings garnished with mint with the mint yoghurt for dipping.

DEEP-FRIED CAMEMBERT
WITH REDCURRANT JELLY

Serves: 4   Preparation time: 10 minutes   Cooking time: 4–5 minutes

INGREDIENTS
4 tbsp redcurrant jelly
4 tbsp plain (all-purpose) flour
1 egg, beaten
75 g / 2 ½ oz / ½ cup panko breadcrumbs
1 Camembert, cut into 8 wedges
sunflower oil for deep-frying
salt and pepper

METHOD

- Put the redcurrant jelly, flour, egg and panko breadcrumbs in 4 separate bowls.

- Dip the Camembert wedges alternately in the jelly, flour, egg and breadcrumbs and shake off any excess.

- Heat the oil in a deep fat fryer, according to the manufacturer's instructions, to a temperature of 180°C / 350F.

- Lower the Camembert in the fryer basket and cook for 4–5 minutes or until crisp and golden brown.

- Tip the Camembert into a bowl lined with kitchen paper to remove any excess oil and serve immediately.

BEER-BATTERED ONION RINGS

Serves: 4   Preparation time: 40 minutes   Cooking time: 3 minutes

INGREDIENTS

1 large onion, peeled
300 ml / 10 ½ fl. oz / 1 ¼ cups milk
200 g / 7 oz / 1 ⅓ cups plain (all-purpose) flour
2 tbsp olive oil
250 ml / 9 fl. oz / 1 cup pale ale
salt and pepper
sunflower oil for deep-frying

METHOD

- Thickly slice the onion, then separate the slices into rings. Soak the onion rings in milk for 30 minutes, then drain well and pat dry with kitchen paper.

- Meanwhile, make the batter. Sieve the flour into a bowl then whisk in the olive oil and ale until smoothly combined. Season with salt and pepper.

- Heat the oil in a deep fat fryer, according to the manufacturer's instructions, to a temperature of 180°C (160°C) / 350F / gas 4.

- Dip the onion rings in the batter, then drop them straight into the hot oil. Fry for 3 minutes or until crisp and brown, then drain well and tip them into a bowl lined with kitchen paper.

- Serve immediately.

KING PRAWN PUFFS

Makes: 12   Preparation time: 20 minutes   Cooking time: 20 minutes

INGREDIENTS

450 g / 1 lb / 1¼ cups all-butter puff pastry
1 egg, beaten
12 raw king prawns, peeled with tails left intact
1 onion, cut into 12 wedges
1 tbsp poppy seeds
1 tbsp sesame seeds
salt and pepper

METHOD

- Preheat the oven to 220°C (200°C fan) / 425F / gas 7.

- Roll out the pastry on a lightly floured surface into a large rectangle, then cut it into 12 strips and brush with egg.

- Lay a king prawn and a wedge of onion at the top of each strip, then roll them up, leaving the prawn tails poking out of the ends.

- Brush the tops with beaten egg and sprinkle with poppy and sesame seeds, then bake for 20 minutes or until golden brown and cooked through.

TUNA PATE

Serves: 4   Preparation time: 10 minutes

INGREDIENTS
4 spring onions (scallions)
125 g / 4 ½ oz / ½ cup canned tuna, flaked
100 g / 3 ½ oz / ½ cup cream cheese
2 tbsp lime juice
salt and pepper

METHOD
- Chop the spring onions and reserve the green ends for garnish.

- Put the white part of the spring onions in a food processor with the tuna, cream cheese and lime juice and season generously with salt and pepper.

- Pulse until smooth and evenly mixed, then taste for seasoning and adjust with extra salt, pepper, or lime juice.

- Spoon into a serving bowl and sprinkle with the reserved spring onion tops.

SPICY KING PRAWN SKEWERS

Serves: 4   Preparation time: 60 minutes   Cooking time: 4 minutes

INGREDIENTS

14 king prawns, peeled with tails intact
3 cloves of garlic, crushed
2 red chillies (chilies), finely chopped
2 tbsp olive oil
vegetable skewers and salad leaves to serve
salt and pepper

METHOD

- Soak 4 wooden skewers in cold water for 20 minutes.

- Lay 7 of the prawns flat on a chopping board, then skewer them with 2 of the skewers. Repeat with the remaining prawns.

- Pound the garlic and chillies to a pulp with a pestle and mortar, then stir in the oil and season with salt and pepper. Brush the mixture over the prawns and leave to marinate for 30 minutes.

- Preheat the grill to its highest setting.

- Grill the prawns for 2 minutes on each side or until they turn pink and opaque. Serve immediately with vegetable skewers and salad leaves.

MOULES MARINIERE

Serves: 4   Preparation time: 5 minutes   Cooking time: 18 minutes

INGREDIENTS

2 tbsp olive oil
2 shallots, finely chopped
2 cloves of garlic, finely chopped
250 ml / 9 fl. oz / 1 cup dry white wine
2 litres / 3 pints 7 fl. oz / 8 cups live
    mussels, scrubbed
150 ml / 5 ½ fl. oz / ⅔ cup double (heavy) cream
2 tbsp flat leaf parsley, finely chopped
salt and pepper

METHOD

- Heat the oil in a large saucepan and fry the shallots and garlic for 5 minutes without colouring. Pour in the wine and heat to boiling, then reduce by half.

- Add the mussels to the pan, cover with a lid, and leave to steam for 6 minutes or until they have all opened, shaking the pan half way through.

- Stir in the cream and parsley, then serve immediately.

SEAFOOD AND AVOCADO COCKTAILS

Makes: 6   Preparation time: 20 minutes

INGREDIENTS

250 g / 9 oz / 1 ⅔ cups sashimi-grade tuna
    loin, diced
2 tbsp soy sauce
1 tsp sesame oil
4 avocados, halved and stoned
2 limes, juiced
1 tsp wasabi paste
150 g / 5 ½ oz / 1 cup cooked crayfish
    tails, peeled
150 g / 5 ½ oz / ¾ cup white crabmeat
18 king prawns
250 g / 9 oz / 1 cup good quality mayonnaise
2 tbsp fresh dill, chopped, plus a few sprigs
    to garnish
Cayenne pepper for sprinkling

METHOD

- Toss the tuna with the soy and sesame oil then divide between six glasses.

- Scrape the avocado flesh out of the skins and put it in a food processor with the lime juice and wasabi paste. Blend to a smooth purée and add salt to taste.

- Spoon the avocado mixture on top of the tuna and top with the crayfish tails and crabmeat.

- Arrange 3 king prawns on top of each cocktail, then pipe or spoon some mayonnaise on top.

- Sprinkle with dill and Cayenne pepper and garnish with some extra sprigs of dill.

SALADS & SOUPS

CARROT AND CUMIN SOUP

Serves: 6   Preparation time: 10 minutes   Cooking time: 25 minutes

INGREDIENTS
2 tbsp olive oil
2 tbsp butter
1 onion, finely chopped
2 cloves of garlic, crushed
2 tsp cumin seeds, plus extra to sprinkle
4 large carrots, diced
1 litre / 1 pint 15 fl. oz / 4 cups vegetable stock
4 tbsp double (heavy) cream
salt and pepper

METHOD
- Heat the oil and butter in a saucepan and fry the onion for 5 minutes or until softened.

- Add the garlic, cumin and carrots to the pan and cook for 2 more minutes, then stir in the stock and heat to boiling.

- Simmer for 15 minutes or until the carrots are tender. Ladle the soup into a liquidiser and blend until smooth, then season to taste with salt and pepper.

- Divide the soup between 6 warm bowls, then drizzle with cream and sprinkle with cumin seeds.

CHICKEN AND CROUTON SALAD

Serves: 4   Preparation time: 10 minutes   Cooking time: 8 minutes

INGREDIENTS

2 thick slices white bread
4 tbsp olive oil
2 cooked chicken breasts, sliced
½ iceberg lettuce, chopped
1 small onion, sliced and separated into rings
2 medium tomatoes, cut into thin wedges
flat leaf parsley to garnish
salt and pepper

For the dressing:

2 tbsp mayonnaise
½ garlic clove, crushed
½ lemon, juiced
2 tbsp olive oil

METHOD

- Preheat the oven to 190°C (170°C fan) / 375F / gas 5.

- To make the dressing, mix the mayonnaise with the garlic, then use a fork to whisk in the lemon juice and olive oil.

- Brush the bread with oil on both sides then cut off and discard the crusts. Cut the bread into cubes and spread them out on a baking tray. Bake the croutons in the oven for 8 minutes or until crisp and golden. Transfer to a wire rack to cool.

- Arrange the chicken, lettuce, onion and tomatoes on 4 plates, then scatter over the croutons. Drizzle with the dressing and garnish with parsley.

TARTIFLETTE SOUP

Serves: 6   Preparation time: 20 minutes   Cooking time: 35 minutes

INGREDIENTS

2 tbsp butter
3 leeks, halved and thickly sliced
2 cloves of garlic, crushed
3 medium potatoes, cubed
1 litre / 1 pint 15 fl. oz / 4 cups ham stock
6 slices Reblochon cheese
salt and pepper

METHOD

- Heat the butter in a large saucepan and fry the leeks over a gentle heat for 10 minutes to soften. Add the garlic and cook for 2 more minutes, then add the potatoes and stock.

- Heat to boiling and simmer for 20 minutes or until the potatoes are tender.

- Blend the soup until smooth in a liquidiser, then taste and adjust the seasoning with salt and pepper.

- Ladle the soup into 6 heatproof bowls and top each one with a slice of Reblochon. Toast the cheese under a hot grill, then serve immediately.

BEER
THE
PUB
BIER
BEOIR
BIER

SALAD NIÇOISE
WITH CODDLED EGGS

Serves: 4   Preparation time: 15 minutes   Cooking time: 15 minutes

INGREDIENTS

450 g / 1 lb / 1 ⅓ cups tuna steak, cut into 12 squares
2 tbsp olive oil
75 g / 2 ½ oz / ⅓ cup marinated anchovy fillets
1 red pepper, very thinly sliced
1 yellow pepper, very thinly sliced
150 g / 5 ½ oz / 1 cup cooked green (string) beans
200 g / 7 oz / 1 cup sun-blush tomatoes
150 g / 5 ½ oz / 1 cup kalamata olives
lemon slices and basil leaves to serve
salt and pepper

For the eggs:

150 ml / 5 ½ fl. oz / ⅔ cup crème fraiche
4 large eggs

METHOD

- Preheat the oven to 180°C (160°C fan) / 350F / gas 4.

- To coddle the eggs, season the crème fraiche well with salt and pepper and divide it between 4 small ovenproof bowls. Make a well in the centre and crack an egg into each one. Season with salt and pepper.

- Sit the bowls in a roasting tin and pour enough boiling water around them to come halfway up the sides. Transfer the tin to the oven and bake for 15 minutes or until the whites of the eggs are set, but the yolks are still runny.

- Meanwhile, brush the tuna with oil and season with salt and pepper, then cook under a hot grill for 2 minutes on each side or until browned, but still pink in the middle.

- Arrange the tuna with the rest of the salad ingredients on four plates and serve with the coddled eggs.

MUSHROOM AND FETA SOUP

Serves: 4   Preparation time: 5 minutes   Cooking time: 25 minutes

INGREDIENTS

2 tbsp olive oil
2 tbsp butter
1 onion, finely chopped
2 cloves of garlic, crushed
400 g / 14 oz / 5 ⅓ cups flat cap
    mushrooms, sliced
1 litre / 1 pint 15 fl. oz / 4 cups vegetable stock
100 ml / 3 ½ fl. oz / ½ cup double (heavy) cream
100 g / 3 ½ oz / ⅔ cup feta, crumbled
salt and pepper

METHOD

* Heat the oil and butter in a saucepan and fry the onion for 5 minutes or until softened.

* Add the garlic and mushrooms to the pan and cook for 5 more minutes, then stir in the vegetable stock and heat to boiling.

* Simmer for 15 minutes then remove a large spoonful of mushrooms with a slotted spoon and reserve.

* Add the cream, then blend the soup until smooth with a liquidiser or stick blender. Taste the soup for seasoning and adjust with salt and pepper, then stir in the reserved mushrooms and crumbled feta.

* Ladle into warm bowls and grind over a little more black pepper.

LIGHT BITES

ong housewives
terior lovers.
ese years ex-
craft tapes
boxes are plent-
t and easily ob-
ody.
y designs of vari
r tapes such
rattan

BEEF GRANARY BAGUETTES

Makes: 4   Preparation time: 5 minutes

INGREDIENTS
2 granary baguettes, halved
4 tbsp tomato purée
4 iceberg lettuce leaves, shredded
100 g / 3 ½ oz / ½ cup chargrilled red peppers
    in oil, drained
150 g / 5 ½ oz / 1 cup cold roast beef,
    thinly sliced
½ red onion, thinly sliced
salt and pepper

METHOD
- Split the baguette halves in half horizontally and spread with the tomato pizza sauce.
- Fill with shredded lettuce and strips of chargrilled peppers, then arrange the beef and onion on top.

BEER
THE
PUB
BIER
BEOIR
BIER

MOZZARELLA AND TOMATO PANINI
WITH PESTO

Serves: 2   Preparation time: 5 minutes   Cooking time: 3 minutes

INGREDIENTS
1 long ciabatta roll, halved
3 tbsp pesto
1 mozzarella ball, sliced
1 medium tomato, sliced
salt and pepper

METHOD
- Put an electric panini press on to heat.

- Open the rolls and fill with the pesto, mozzarella and tomato.

- Toast the panini for 3 minutes or according to the manufacturer's instructions.

- Cut in half and serve immediately.

TUNA FISHCAKES

Serves: 6   Preparation time: 25 minutes   Cooking time: 4–5 minutes

INGREDIENTS

4 tbsp plain (all-purpose) flour
1 egg, beaten
75 g / 2 ½ oz / ½ cup panko breadcrumbs
450 g / 1 lb / 2 cups leftover mashed potato
200 g / 7 oz / 1 ⅓ cups canned tuna in
    oil, drained
2 tbsp dill, finely chopped
2 tsp Dijon mustard
sunflower oil for deep-frying
rocket (arugula) and lemon wedges to serve
salt and pepper

METHOD

* Put the flour, egg and panko breadcrumbs in three separate bowls.

* Mix the mashed potato with the tuna, dill and mustard and season to taste with salt and pepper. Shape the mixture into 12 patties, then dip them alternately in the flour, egg and breadcrumbs and shake off any excess.

* Heat the oil in a deep fat fryer, according to the manufacturer's instructions, to a temperature of 180°C / 350F.

* Lower the fishcakes in the fryer basket and cook for 4–5 minutes or until crisp and golden brown. Tip the fishcakes into a kitchen-paper-lined bowl to remove any excess oil.

* Serve hot with rocket leaves and lemon wedges on the side.

OLIVE OIL AND GARLIC BRUSCHETTA

Serves: 4   Preparation time: 2 minutes   Cooking time: 2–3 minutes

INGREDIENTS
4 slices rustic bread
1 clove of garlic, halved
4 tbsp extra virgin olive oil
salt and pepper

METHOD
- Toast the bread in a toaster or under a hot grill until golden brown.

- Rub the bread vigorously with the cut side of the garlic clove, then drizzle with oil and season lightly with salt and pepper. Serve immediately.

STEAKS & BURGERS

VEGETABLE BURGERS
WITH GOATS' CHEESE

Serves: 4   Preparation time: 30 minutes   Cooking time: 10 minutes   Chilling time: 2 hours

INGREDIENTS

250 g / 9 oz / 2 cups red lentils
2 spring onions (scallions), finely chopped
2 cloves of garlic, crushed
1 tsp ground cumin
1 tsp ground coriander seeds
100 g / 3 ½ oz / ⅔ cup gram flour
1 courgette (zucchini), grated
1 carrot, grated
2 tablespoons sunflower oil
4 sesame burger buns, split in half horizontally
12 slices goats' cheese
salt and pepper

METHOD

- Cook the lentils in boiling water for 20 minutes or until tender, then drain well.

- Put the lentils in a food processor with the spring onions, garlic, spices and gram flour and pulse until evenly mixed. Put the grated courgette in a clean tea towel, then bring up the edges, twist and squeeze to get rid of any excess moisture. Stir the courgette into the lentil mixture with the grated carrot and season with salt and pepper.

- Shape the mixture into 4 burgers, then chill in the fridge for 2 hours.

- Heat the oil in a large frying pan, then fry the burgers for 5 minutes on each side or until golden brown.

- Lay the burgers on the bun bases and top each one with 3 slices of goats' cheese. Toast under a hot grill to lightly brown the cheese, then replace the bun tops and serve.

CRISPY FISH BURGERS

Serves: 4   Preparation time: 15 minutes   Cooking time: 15 minutes

INGREDIENTS

4 tbsp plain (all-purpose) flour
1 egg, beaten
75 g / 2 ½ oz / ½ cup panko breadcrumbs
4 small portions of pollock fillet
sunflower oil for deep-frying
4 bread rolls, halved horizontally
4 tbsp tartar sauce
salt and pepper
lemon wedges to serve

METHOD

- Put the flour, egg and panko breadcrumbs in 3 separate bowls. Dip the fish first in the flour, then in the egg, then in the breadcrumbs.

- Heat the oil in a deep fat fryer, according to the manufacturer's instructions, to a temperature of 180°C / 350F.

- Lower the fish in the fryer basket and cook for 5 minutes or until crisp and golden brown. Line a large bowl with a thick layer of kitchen paper and when they are ready, tip the fish burgers into the bowl to remove any excess oil.

- Spread the bun bases with tartar sauce, then top with the fish and replace the lids. Serve immediately with lemon wedges.

BEER
THE
PUB
BIER
BEOIR
BIER
★ ★ ★

MAXI HAMBURGERS

Serves: 4   Preparation time: 45 minutes   Cooking time: 12 minutes

INGREDIENTS

450 g / 1 lb / 3 cups beef mince
2 tbsp double (heavy) cream
1 tsp Dijon mustard
4 tbsp sunflower oil
8 rashers smoked streaky bacon
4 slices Roquefort
4 large eggs
4 crusty rolls, halved
4 tbsp red onion marmalade
4 lettuce leaves
4 slices tomato
2 dill pickles, sliced
salt and pepper

METHOD

- Mix the beef with the cream and mustard and season generously with salt and pepper, then knead lightly until sticky. Divide the mixture into four and squeeze each piece into a tight patty. Make a slight hollow in the centre of each side as they will bulge when cooking. Chill in the fridge for 30 minutes.

- Heat half of the oil in a frying pan then fry the burgers for 8 minutes, turning every 2 minutes. Meanwhile, cook the bacon under a hot grill until crisp.

- When the burgers are ready, turn off the heat, top with the Roquefort and cover the pan with a lid while you cook the eggs.

- Heat the rest of the oil in a frying pan and fry the eggs for 4 minutes or until the whites are set, but the yolks are still a bit soft.

- Spread the bottom half of each roll with onion marmalade and top with the lettuce and tomato. Sit the burgers on top and add a few slices of dill pickle and the bacon. Position the eggs on top and serve with the tops of the buns on the side.

TURKEY BURGERS

Serves: 4   Preparation time: 25 minutes   Cooking time: 8 minutes

INGREDIENTS

450 g / 1 lb / 2 cups turkey breast, cubed
1 clove of garlic, crushed
1 tbsp lemon zest, finely grated
25 g / 1 oz / ¼ cup Parmesan, finely grated
2 tbsp olive oil
2 tomatoes, diced
1 small onion, finely chopped
2 tbsp flat leaf parsley, chopped
4 sesame buns, split in half
2 tbsp tomato ketchup
salt and pepper

METHOD

- Put the turkey, garlic, lemon zest and Parmesan in a food processor and pulse until finely chopped and evenly mixed. Shape the mixture into 4 patties and chill in the freezer for 15 minutes to firm up.

- Meanwhile, heat a cast iron griddle pan on the hob until smoking hot. Brush the burgers with oil then griddle for 4 minutes on each side or until nicely marked and cooked through.

- While the burgers are cooking, mix the tomato, onion and parsley together and season with salt and pepper to make a salsa.

- Spread the bottom half of the buns with ketchup, then position the burgers on top and spoon over the salsa. Sit the bun tops on top and serve immediately.

STEAK TAGLIATA
WITH ROCKET

Serves: 2   Preparation time: 15 minutes   Cooking time: 7 minutes

INGREDIENTS
225 g / 8 oz / ¾ cup rump steak
1 tbsp butter
50 g / 1 ¾ oz / 2 cups rocket (arugula) leaves
balsamic vinegar to dress
salt and pepper

METHOD
- Preheat the oven to 200°C (180°C fan) / 400F / gas 6 and put a frying pan on to heat for 5 minutes or until smoking hot.
- Trim the beef of any fat and dry it really well with kitchen paper. Season the steak liberally with sea salt and black pepper, then transfer it to the frying pan.
- Allow it to cook, without disturbing, for 3 minutes, then turn it over, add the knob of butter and transfer the pan to the oven for 4 minutes.
- Move the beef to a warm plate, wrap with a double layer of foil and leave to rest for 5 minutes.
- Arrange the rocket on a wooden board. When the steak has rested, cut it into thick slices and arrange on top of the rocket. Serve with balsamic vinegar on the side for drizzling over.

ROSE VEAL STEAKS
WITH CAMBOZOLA

Serves: 2   Preparation time: 15 minutes   Cooking time: 7 minutes

INGREDIENTS
2 x 225 g / 8 oz / ½ cup rose veal fillet steaks
1 tbsp butter
2 slices Cambozola cheese

For the salad:
75 g / 2 ½ oz / ⅓ cup red seedless
    grapes, halved
75 g / 2 ½ oz / ⅓ cup green seedless
    grapes, halved
a handful of lamb's lettuce
2 tbsp hazelnuts (cobnuts), roughly chopped
2 tbsp hazelnut oil
salt and pepper

METHOD
- Preheat the oven to 200°C (180°C fan) / 400F / gas 6 and put a frying pan on to heat for 5 minutes or until smoking hot.

- Dry the veal really well with kitchen paper, then season liberally with sea salt and black pepper.

- Transfer the steaks to the frying pan and cook without disturbing for 3 minutes. Turn them over, add the butter and transfer the pan to the oven for 4 minutes.

- Move the steaks to a warm plate, top with the cheese and leave to rest for 5 minutes.

- Toss the grapes with the lamb's lettuce and hazelnuts and dress with the oil and a little salt and pepper. Serve with the steaks.

CLASSIC DISHES

INDIVIDUAL FISH PIES

Serves: 6   Preparation time: 45 minutes   Cooking time: 20 minutes

INGREDIENTS

450 g / 1 lb / 1 ¼ cups potatoes, peeled and cubed
500 ml / 17 ½ fl. oz / 2 cups milk
1 bay leaf
400 g / 14 oz / 1 ½ cups smoked haddock fillet
4 tbsp butter
2 tbsp plain (all-purpose) flour
salt and pepper

METHOD

- Preheat the oven to 200°C (180°C fan) / 400F / gas 6.

- Cook the potatoes in boiling salted water for 12 minutes or until tender then drain well.

- Meanwhile, put the milk and bay leaf in a small saucepan and bring to a simmer. Lay the haddock in a snugly-fitting dish and pour the hot milk over the top. Cover the dish with cling film and leave to stand for 10 minutes.

- Heat half of the butter in a small saucepan and stir in the flour. Reserve 2 tbsp of the haddock milk for the potatoes and strain the rest into the butter and flour mixture, stirring constantly. Cook until the sauce is thick and smooth.

- Remove any skin and bones from the haddock then flake the flesh into the white sauce. Season to taste with salt and black pepper then divide the mixture between 6 individual pie dishes. Mash the potatoes with the reserved milk and remaining butter and spoon it on top of the haddock.

- Bake the pies for 20 minutes or until the topping is golden brown.

ASPARAGUS AND LEMON RISOTTO

Serves: 2   Preparation time: 5 minutes   Cooking time: 25 minutes

INGREDIENTS

1 litre / 1 pint 15 fl. oz / 4 cups good quality
    vegetable stock
2 tbsp olive oil
1 onion, finely chopped
2 cloves of garlic, crushed
1 lemon, zest finely pared
150 g / 5 ½ oz / ¾ cup risotto rice
100 g / 3 ½ oz / ½ cup asparagus spears,
    cut into short lengths
2 tbsp butter
salt and pepper

METHOD

- Heat the stock in a saucepan and keep it just below simmering point.
- Heat the olive oil in a sauté pan and gently fry the onion for 5 minutes without browning. Add the garlic and most of the lemon zest and cook for 2 more minutes then stir in the rice.
- When it is well coated with the oil, add the asparagus, followed by 2 ladles of the hot stock. Cook, stirring occasionally, until most of the stock has been absorbed before adding the next two ladles. Continue in this way for around 15 minutes or until the rice is just tender.
- Stir in the butter, then cover the pan and take off the heat to rest for 4 minutes. Uncover the pan and season well with salt and pepper, then spoon into warm bowls and top with the remaining lemon zest.

CRUSTED COD
WITH LEEKS

Serves: 4   Preparation time: 15 minutes   Cooking time: 20 minutes

INGREDIENTS
2 tbsp butter
3 leeks, julienned
4 tbsp breadcrumbs
4 tbsp flaked (slivered) almonds
4 tbsp Parmesan, finely grated
4 portions of cod fillet, skinned
2 tbsp Dijon mustard
2 tbsp chives, chopped
salt and pepper

METHOD
- Preheat the oven to 190°C (170°C fan) / 375F / gas 5.
- Melt the butter in a frying pan then fry the leeks for 10 minutes or until softened.
- Meanwhile, mix the breadcrumbs with the almonds and Parmesan. Spread the cod with mustard, then pack the breadcrumb mixture on top.
- Season the leeks with salt and pepper, then transfer them to a baking dish and arrange the cod on top in a single layer. Transfer the dish to the oven and bake for 20 minutes or until the cod is just cooked in the centre and the topping is golden brown.
- Sprinkle with chopped chives and serve immediately.

BEER
BIER
THE
PUB
BEOIR
BIER
★ ★ ★

SPEEDY SAUSAGE LASAGNE

Serves: 6   Preparation time: 10 minutes   Cooking time: 30 minutes

INGREDIENTS
24 fresh lasagne sheets
300 g / 10 ½ oz / 2 cups Italian-style
  sausages, sliced
400 g / 14 oz / 2 ⅔ cups canned tomatoes,
  drained and chopped
3 mozzarella balls, thinly sliced
2 tbsp Parmesan, finely grated
salt and pepper

METHOD
- Preheat the oven to 190°C (170°C fan) / 375F / gas 5.
- Layer up the lasagne sheets, sausage slices, tomatoes and mozzarella inside 6 individual baking dishes, finishing with a layer of mozzarella.
- Sprinkle with Parmesan and bake for 30 minutes or until piping hot all the way to the centres.

PEA AND ASPARAGUS LASAGNE

Serves: 6   Preparation time: 15 minutes   Cooking time: 1 hour

INGREDIENTS

2 tbsp butter
2 cloves of garlic, crushed
2 tbsp plain (all-purpose) flour
600 ml / 1 pint / 2 ½ cups vegetable stock
100 ml / 3 ½ fl. oz / ½ cup double (heavy) cream
12 asparagus spears, cut into short lengths
200 g / 7 oz / 1 ⅓ cups frozen peas, defrosted
2 tbsp flat leaf parsley, finely chopped
1 tbsp mint leaves, finely chopped
1 tbsp thyme leaves
400 g / 14 oz / 2 cups dried lasagne sheets
4 tbsp Parmesan, finely grated
salt and pepper

METHOD

- Preheat the oven to 200°C (180°C fan) / 400F / gas 6.

- Melt the butter in a small saucepan and fry the garlic for 30 seconds. Stir in the flour then gradually incorporate the stock and cream, stirring continuously to avoid any lumps forming.

- Simmer the sauce until it thickens, then season to taste with salt and pepper. Set aside a ladle of the sauce, then stir the asparagus, peas and herbs into the rest and simmer for 2 more minutes.

- Layer up the lasagne sheets with the vegetables in a greased baking dish, finishing with a layer of lasagne.

- Pour the reserved sauce over the top and sprinkle with Parmesan, then bake the lasagne for 45 minutes or until the top is golden brown and the pasta is tender all the way through.

BARBECUE BABY BACK RIBS

Serves: 4   Preparation time: 4 hours 30 minutes   Cooking time: 3 hours

INGREDIENTS

2 tbsp olive oil
1 small onion, grated
3 cloves of garlic, crushed
1 tbsp ginger, finely grated
1 tsp mixed spice
200 ml / 7 fl. oz / ¾ cup tomato passata
200 ml / 7 fl. oz / ¾ cup apple juice
salt and pepper
3 tbsp dark brown sugar
1 ½ lemons, juiced
1 tbsp Worcestershire sauce
1 tbsp Dijon mustard
2 racks of baby back pork ribs,
    membrane removed
potato salad to serve

METHOD

- Heat the oil in a saucepan and fry the onion, garlic and ginger for 3 minutes without browning. Stir in the mixed spice then add the passata, apple juice, sugar, lemon juice, Worcestershire sauce and mustard with a large pinch of salt and bring to the boil.

- Turn down the heat and simmer for 10 minutes or until the sauce is thick and smooth.

- Leave the sauce to cool, then brush half of it over the ribs and leave to marinate in the fridge for 4 hours or overnight.

- Preheat the oven to 110°C (90°C fan) / 225F / gas ¼.

- Transfer the ribs to a roasting tin and slow-roast for 3 hours, turning occasionally and basting with the rest of the sauce.

- The ribs can either be served straight away or cooked over a hot charcoal barbecue for a few minutes to give a smoky taste.

- Serve with potato salad.

TAPENADE GRIDDLED CHICKEN BREASTS

Serves: 4   Preparation time: 1 hour 5 minutes   Cooking time: 12 minutes

INGREDIENTS
4 tbsp black olive tapenade
1 clove of garlic, crushed
2 tbsp olive oil
4 skinless chicken breasts
1 tbsp Parmesan, grated
potato wedges and baby spinach leaves to serve
salt and pepper

METHOD
- Mix the tapenade with the garlic and oil, then rub it over the chicken breasts and leave to marinate for 1 hour.
- Heat a griddle pan until smoking hot, then griddle the chicken for 12 minutes or until cooked through, turning every 3 minutes.
- Sprinkle with Parmesan and serve with potato wedges and baby spinach leaves.

GRILLED LAMB CHOPS

WITH HERB OIL

Serves: 2   Preparation time: 5 minutes   Cooking time: 8 minutes

INGREDIENTS

8 small lamb chops
3 tbsp olive oil
1 clove of garlic, finely chopped
1 tbsp flat leaf parsley, finely chopped
1 tbsp young thyme leaves, finely chopped
roast potatoes and tomato salsa to serve
salt and pepper

METHOD

- Preheat the grill to its highest setting.
- Brush the lamb chops with 1 tbsp of the oil and season liberally with salt and pepper. Cook the lamb under the grill for 8 minutes, turning occasionally, or until cooked to your liking.
- Meanwhile, stir the garlic and herbs into the rest of the oil. Season with salt and pepper, then spoon the mixture over the lamb when it's ready.
- Serve with roast potatoes and tomato salsa.

THAI RED CHICKEN AND CURRY
WITH CUCUMBER & DILL RICE SALAD

Serves: 2   Preparation time: 2 minutes   Cooking time: 10 minutes

INGREDIENTS
400 ml / 14 fl. oz / 1 ⅔ cups coconut milk
100 ml / 3 ½ fl. oz / ½ cup chicken stock
2 tbsp red Thai curry paste
1 red chilli (chili), thinly sliced
2 kaffir lime leaves
1 tbsp fish sauce
1 tsp caster (superfine) sugar
150 g / 5 ½ oz / ¾ cup skinless chicken
    breast, cubed
½ red pepper, sliced
75 g / 2 ½ oz / ½ cup green beans, halved
2 shallots, sliced
75 g / 2 ½ oz / ½ cup baby corn
1 small courgette (zucchini), halved and sliced
coriander (cilantro) leaves to garnish
salt and pepper

METHOD

- Heat the coconut milk and stock together in a saucepan, then stir in the curry paste to dissolve. Add the chilli and kaffir lime leaves and bring to a simmer.

- Stir in the fish sauce and sugar then taste it and adjust the levels.

- Add the chicken breast to the pan and poach gently for 2 minutes, then add the vegetables and simmer for 4 minutes.

- Ladle into 4 warm bowls and serve garnished with coriander.

SAUSAGE AND TOMATO PASTA SAUCE

Serves: 4   Preparation time: 5 minutes   Cooking time: 35 minutes

INGREDIENTS
2 tbsp olive oil
300 g / 10 ½ oz / 2 cups small
    Italian-style sausages
1 onion, finely chopped
2 cloves of garlic, finely chopped
1 red pepper, diced
1 tsp dried Italian herbs
75 g / 2 ½ oz / 1 cup mushrooms, sliced
12 cherry tomatoes
4 tbsp Marsala
400 g / 14 oz / 2 ⅔ cups tomato passata
a big handful of basil leaves
penne to serve
salt and pepper

METHOD
- Heat the oil in a large cast iron casserole dish and brown the sausages all over. Remove from the pan and add the onion, garlic and pepper and fry for 5 minutes.

- Add the herbs, mushrooms and tomatoes to the pan with the sausages, then pour in the Marsala and bubble until it has almost entirely evaporated.

- Stir in the passata, then simmer for 20 minutes. Taste the sauce and adjust the seasoning with salt and pepper, then stir in the basil leaves. Serve with freshly cooked penne pasta.

STEAK AND KIDNEY POT PIES

Serves: 6   Preparation time: 2 hours 15 minutes   Cooking time: 30 minutes

INGREDIENTS

4 tbsp olive oil
900 g / 2 lb / 6 cups braising steak, cubed
4 lamb's kidneys, trimmed and cubed
1 onion, finely chopped
3 cloves of garlic, finely chopped
2 bay leaves
600 ml / 1 pint / 2 ½ cups good quality
    beef stock
250 g / 9 oz / 3 cups mushrooms, quartered
225 g / 8 oz / ¾ cup all-butter puff pastry
1 egg, beaten
salt and pepper

METHOD

- Heat the oil in an oven-proof saucepan and sear the steak and kidney in batches until well browned. Remove the meat from the pan, add the onions, garlic and bay and cook for 5 minutes.

- Pour in the stock and return the beef and kidneys, then simmer for 2 hours.

- 30 minutes before the end of the cooking time, season to taste with salt and pepper and stir in the mushrooms. Leave to cool completely, then divide the filling between 6 individual pie dishes.

- Preheat the oven to 220°C (200°C fan) / 425F / gas 7.

- Roll out the pastry and cut out 6 circles a little larger in diameter than the top of the pie dishes. Lay the pastry on top of the filling and brush with beaten egg.

- Bake the pies for 30 minutes or until the pastry is golden brown and cooked through.

PORK CHOPS
WITH SAGE BUTTER AND ROSTI

Serves: 4   Preparation time: 1 hour 30 minutes   Cooking time: 15 minutes

INGREDIENTS

4 pork chops, French-trimmed
2 tbsp olive oil
75 g / 2 ½ oz / ⅓ cup butter, softened
1 clove of garlic, crushed
1 tbsp sage leaves, finely chopped
baby spinach leaves to serve
salt and pepper

For the rosti

450 g / 1 lb / 2 ½ cup waxy potatoes
1 shallot, thinly sliced
1 tsp Dijon mustard
1 large egg white
2 tbsp butter

METHOD

- To make the rosti, cook the unpeeled potatoes in boiling water for 18 minutes or until a skewer slides in easily. Drain well, then leave to cool completely before peeling.

- Coarsely grate the potatoes, then stir in the shallots. Whisk the mustard into the egg white and season with salt and pepper, then stir it into the potatoes. Shape the mixture into 4 flat patties then chill for 30 minutes.

- Melt the butter in a frying pan then fry each rosti over a low heat for 15 minutes, turning halfway through.

- Meanwhile, brush the chops with oil and season with salt and pepper, then cook under a hot grill for 4 minutes on each side or until cooked through.

- Mix the softened butter with the garlic and sage, then spoon it on top of the chops. Serve with the rosti and some baby spinach leaves.

CHICKEN AND CARROT POT PIES

Serves: 4   Preparation time: 1 hour   Cooking time: 30 minutes

INGREDIENTS
2 tbsp butter
1 onion, chopped
2 carrots, chopped
1 tsp plain (all-purpose) flour
250 ml / 9 fl. oz / 1 cup milk
200 g / 7 oz / 1 cup cooked chicken breast, cubed
½ tbsp fresh thyme leaves
salt and pepper

For the pastry:
100 g / 3 ½ oz / ½ cup butter, frozen
200 g / 7 oz / 1 ½ cups plain (all-purpose) flour
1 egg, beaten
thyme sprigs to garnish

METHOD
- To make the flaky pastry, grate the frozen butter into the flour and add a pinch of salt. Stir in just enough cold water to bring the pastry together into a pliable dough then chill for 30 minutes.

- Preheat the oven to 200°C (180°C fan) / 400F / gas 6.

- Heat the butter in a saucepan and fry the onion and carrot for 5 minutes without browning. Sprinkle in the flour and stir well, then stir in the milk and bubble until it thickens slightly. Add the chicken and thyme and heat through, then season to taste with salt and white pepper.

- Roll out the pastry on a lightly floured surface and cut out 4 circles. Divide the filling between 4 individual pie dishes and brush the rims with water. Top each pie with a pastry lid and crimp the edges to seal. Brush the tops with beaten egg.

- Bake the pies for 30 minutes or until the pastry is golden brown. Garnish with thyme sprigs before serving.

SAUSAGES
WITH POLENTA PATTIES

Serves: 4   Preparation time: 45 minutes   Cooking time: 20 minutes

INGREDIENTS
225 g / 8 oz / 2 ½ cups instant polenta
75 g / 2 ½ oz / ⅓ cup butter
75 g / 2 ½ oz / ¾ cup Parmesan, finely grated
2 tbsp olive oil
8 Italian-style pork sausages
salt and pepper

METHOD
- Bring 1 litre of water to the boil with a large pinch of salt then stir in the polenta.
- Continue to cook, stirring continuously, until the polenta is very thick.
- Beat in the butter and three quarters of the Parmesan, then leave the mixture to cool a little. When the polenta is cool enough to handle, but before it sets hard, shape it into 8 burgers. Chill in the fridge for 15 minutes to set.
- Heat the oil in a large frying pan then fry the sausages over a gentle heat for 15 minutes, turning occasionally. Transfer the sausages to a plate and keep warm.
- Fry the burgers in the sausage pan over a higher heat for 3 minutes on each side or until golden brown. Serve with the sausages.

PAN-FRIED SALMON

Serves: 4   Preparation time: 5 minutes   Cooking time: 10 minutes

INGREDIENTS

4 portions salmon fillet
½ tsp pink peppercorns, lightly crushed
4 tbsp olive oil
50 g / 1 ¾ oz / 2 cups mixed salad leaves
½ carrot, coarsely grated
3 radishes, sliced
a few sprigs of dill
½ lemon
salt and pepper

METHOD

- Dry the salmon well with kitchen paper, then season with salt and pink peppercorns.

- Heat half of the oil in a large frying pan, then fry the salmon skin side down for 5 minutes.

- Turn the salmon over and cook for 1 minute, then turn off the heat and leave to cook in the residual heat of the pan for 4 minutes.

- Mix the salad leaves with the carrot, radishes and dill and divide between 4 plates. Dress with the rest of the oil and a squeeze of lemon.

- Remove the skin from the salmon fillets and lay them next to the salad on the plates.

KNUCKLE OF PORK
WITH POTATO WEDGES

Serves: 4   Preparation time: 5 minutes   Cooking time: 50 minutes

INGREDIENTS
4 tbsp olive oil
800 g / 1 lb 12 oz / 2 cups medium potatoes,
    cut into wedges
1 tbsp thyme leaves
1 large pork knuckle
salt and pepper

METHOD

- Preheat the oven to 190°C (170°C fan) / 375F / gas 5.

- Put the oil in a large roasting tin and heat in the oven for 5 minutes.

- Carefully tip the potato wedges into the pan and turn to coat in the oil, then sprinkle with thyme and season well with salt and black pepper.

- Sit the pork knuckle on top and bake for 45 minutes, turning the wedges every 15 minutes, until golden brown on the outside and fluffy within.

- Cut the pork into thick slices and serve with the wedges.

FISH AND CHIPS

Serves: 4   Preparation time: 1 hour 45 minutes   Cooking time: 25 minutes

INGREDIENTS

200 g / 7 oz / 1 ⅓ cups plain (all-purpose)
2 tbsp olive oil
250 ml / 9 fl. oz / 1 cup pale ale
8 pollock goujons
ketchup and mushy peas to serve
salt and pepper

For the chips:

4 large Maris Piper potatoes, peeled and cut
    into chips
sunflower oil for deep-frying

METHOD

- Soak the potatoes in cold water for 1 hour to reduce the starch. Drain the chips and dry completely with a clean tea towel, then air-dry on a wire rack for 30 minutes.

- Meanwhile, make the batter. Sieve the flour into a bowl then whisk in the olive oil and ale until smoothly combined.

- Heat the sunflower oil in a deep fat fryer, according to the manufacturer's instructions, to a temperature of 130°C / 275F.

- Par-cook the chips for 10 minutes so that they cook all the way through but don't brown. Drain the chips on plenty of kitchen paper to absorb the excess oil.

- Increase the fryer temperature to 180°C / 350F. Dip the fish in the batter and fry for 4 minutes or until golden brown. Transfer the fish to a kitchen paper lined bowl and increase the fryer temperature to 190°C / 375F.

- Return the chips to the fryer basket and cook for 4–5 minutes or until crisp and golden brown. Drain the chips of excess oil and serve with the fish immediately.

LINGUINI ALLA CARBONARA

Serves: 2   Preparation time: 5 minutes   Cooking time: 12 minutes

INGREDIENTS
200 g / 7 oz / 1 cup dried linguini
4 thick rashers pancetta, diced
2 tbsp thyme sprigs
2 tbsp olive oil
1 clove of garlic, crushed
1 large egg
50 g / 1 ¾ oz / ½ cup Parmesan, finely grated
salt and pepper

METHOD
- Bring a large pan of salted water to the boil and cook the linguini according to the packet instructions or until al dente.
- While the pasta is cooking, fry the pancetta and thyme in the oil for 4 minutes or until golden brown. Add the garlic and cook for 2 more minutes then turn off the heat.
- Beat the egg and stir in half the grated Parmesan with a good grind of black pepper.
- When the linguini is ready, reserve a ladleful of the cooking water and drain the rest. Tip the linguini into the bacon pan and pour in the egg mixture. Mix it all together, adding enough of the cooking water to make a thick shiny sauce that clings to the pasta.
- Divide between 2 warm bowls and sprinkle over the rest of the Parmesan, some parsley and some more black pepper.

CHILLI CON CARNE

Serves: 4   Preparation time: 5 minutes   Cooking time: 1 hour 10 minutes

INGREDIENTS

2 tbsp olive oil
1 onion, finely chopped
2 carrots, cut into chunks
2 dried green chillies (chilies)
2 cloves of garlic, crushed
½ tsp Cayenne pepper
450 g / 1 lb / 2 cups minced beef
400 g / 14 oz / 1 ¾ cups canned
    tomatoes, chopped
200 ml / 7 fl. oz / ¾ cup beef stock
400 g / 14 oz / 1 ¾ cups canned kidney
    beans, drained
plain flour tortillas to serve
salt and pepper

METHOD

- Heat the oil in a large saucepan and fry the onion, carrots and dried chillies for 3 minutes, stirring occasionally.
- Add the garlic and Cayenne and cook for 2 minutes, then add the mince.
- Fry the mince until it starts to brown then add the chopped tomatoes, stock and kidney beans and bring to a gentle simmer.
- Cook the chilli con carne for 1 hour, stirring occasionally, until the mince is tender and the sauce has thickened a little.
- Taste for seasoning and add salt and freshly ground black pepper as necessary.
- Serve with plain flour tortillas.

BEEF STROGANOFF

Serves: 4   Preparation time: 5 minutes   Cooking time: 35 minutes

INGREDIENTS

4 tbsp butter
450 g / 1 lb fillet of beef, thinly sliced
2 onions, sliced
150 g / 5 ½ oz / 2 cups button mushrooms, sliced
1 tsp Hungarian paprika
250 ml / 9 fl. oz / 1 cup soured cream
flat leaf parsley to garnish
salt and pepper

METHOD

- Heat half the butter in a wide sauté pan then sear the steak slices on both sides. Transfer to a warm plate.

- Add the rest of the butter to the pan and fry the onions over a medium heat for 10 minutes to soften. Add the mushrooms and cook for a further 10 minutes, stirring occasionally.

- Turn up the heat, sprinkle in the paprika and cook for 1 more minute, then pour in the soured cream and bring to a simmer.

- Season to taste with salt and pepper, then return the steak to the pan and heat through. Serve garnished with parsley.

SPAGHETTI WITH QUICK COOK RAGU

Serves: 4   Preparation time: 5 minutes   Cooking time: 25 minutes

INGREDIENTS
2 tbsp olive oil
1 onion, finely chopped
2 cloves of garlic, crushed
250 g / 9 oz / 1 ¼ cups minced beef
400 g / 14 oz / 1 ¾ cups canned tomatoes,
    chopped
400 g / 14 oz dried spaghetti
a handful of basil leaves
salt and pepper

METHOD
- Heat the oil in a large saucepan and fry the onion for 5 minutes, stirring occasionally. Add the garlic and cook for 2 minutes, then add the mince.

- Fry the mince until it starts to brown then add the chopped tomatoes and simmer while you cook the spaghetti. Season to taste with salt and pepper.

- Boil the pasta in salted water according to the packet instructions or until al dente. Drain the pasta and stir it into the ragu, then divide between four warm bowls.

- Garnish with basil leaves and serve immediately.

DESSERTS

BREAD AND BUTTER PUDDINGS

Makes: 4   Preparation time: 20 minutes   Cooking time: 1 hour

INGREDIENTS
4 thick slices white bread
3 tbsp butter, softened
4 tbsp sultanas
250 ml / 9 fl. oz / 1 cup milk
200 ml / 7 fl. oz / ¾ cup double (heavy) cream
4 large egg yolks
75 g / 2 ½ oz / ⅓ cup caster (superfine) sugar
1 lemon, zest finely grated
nutmeg to grate

METHOD
- Spread the bread with butter and cut each piece into 4 triangles. Butter 4 small baking dishes and layer up the bread inside with the sultanas.
- Whisk the milk, cream, eggs, sugar and lemon zest together and divide it between the dishes, then leave to soak for 10 minutes.
- Preheat the oven to 150°C (130°C fan) / 300F / gas 2. Bake the puddings for 1 hour or until the custard is just set with a slight wobble. Grate over a little nutmeg and serve hot or cold.

RASPBERRY TRIFLE POTS

Makes: 6   Preparation time: 20 minutes   Cooking time: 10 minutes

INGREDIENTS
200 g / 7 oz / 2 ⅔ cups sponge cake, crumbled
4 tbsp sherry
150 g / 5 ½ oz / 1 cup raspberries
300 ml / 10 ½ fl. oz / 1 ¼ cups double (heavy)
    cream, whipped

For the custard:
450 ml / 12 ½ fl. oz / 1 ¾ cups whole milk
1 vanilla pod, split lengthways
4 large egg yolks
75 g / 2 ½ oz / ⅓ cup caster (superfine) sugar
1 tsp cornflour (cornstarch)

METHOD
- First make the custard. Heat the milk with the vanilla pod, but do not let it boil. Whisk the egg yolks with the caster sugar and cornflour until thick.

- Gradually incorporate the hot milk, whisking all the time, then scrape the mixture back into the saucepan. Stir the custard over a low heat until it thickens then sit the bottom of the pan in a bowl of cold water to stop the cooking.

- Mix the cake crumbs with the sherry and divide half between 6 dessert glasses. Top with half of the whipped cream and half of the raspberries, then spoon over half of the custard.

- Repeat to form a second layer of everything, then serve immediately.

TIRAMISU GATEAU

Serves: 6   Preparation time: 30 minutes   Chilling time: 4 hours

INGREDIENTS

600 ml / 1 pint / 2 ½ cups double (heavy) cream
300 g / 10 ½ oz / 1 ⅓ cups mascarpone
4 tbsp icing (confectioners') sugar
100 ml / 3 ½ fl. oz / ½ cup Marsala
100 ml / 3 ½ fl. oz / ½ cup strong filter
    coffee, cooled
300 g / 10 ½ oz / 3 cups sponge fingers
unsweetened cocoa powder for dusting

METHOD

- Line a deep 20 cm (8 in) round spring-form cake tin with cling film.

- Put the cream, mascarpone and sugar in a bowl with half of the Marsala and whip with an electric whisk until it holds its shape.

- Mix the rest of the Marsala with the coffee. Dip the sponge fingers in the coffee mixture, then arrange them in the bottom of the tin to form an even layer.

- Spoon the cream mixture into a piping bag fitted with a large plain nozzle and pipe it over the top in small blobs.

- Sprinkle the tiramisu with cocoa powder, then refrigerate for 4 hours to set the cream and allow the flavours to develop.

- Carefully unmould the gateau and peel away the cling film before slicing and serving.

APPLE AND BRAMBLE CRUMBLE

Serves: 6   Preparation time: 10 minutes   Cooking time: 40 minutes

INGREDIENTS

2 apples, peeled, cored and sliced
225 g / 8 oz / 1 ½ cups blackberries
225 g / 8 oz / 1 ½ cups raspberries
4 tbsp caster (superfine) sugar
75 g / 2 ½ oz / ⅓ cup butter
50 g / 1 ¾ oz / ⅓ cup plain (all-purpose) flour
25 g / 1 oz / ¼ cup ground almonds
40 g / 1 ½ oz / ¼ cup light brown sugar
whipped cream to serve

METHOD

- Preheat the oven to 180°C (160°C fan) / 350F / gas 4.
- Mix the apples, blackberries and raspberries with the sugar and arrange in the bottom of a baking dish.
- Rub the butter into the flour and stir in the ground almonds and brown sugar.
- Squeeze a handful of the mixture into a clump and then crumble it over the fruit. Use up the rest of the topping in the same way, then shake the dish to level the top.
- Bake the crumble for 40 minutes or until the topping is golden brown and the fruit is bubbling. Serve warm with whipped cream.

REDCURRANT CHEESECAKE

Serves: 10-12   Preparation time: 25 minutes   Cooking time: 50 minutes   Chilling time: 2 hours

INGREDIENTS

200 g / 7 oz / ¾ cup digestive biscuits, crushed
50 g / 1 ¾ oz / ¼ cup butter, melted
600 g / 1 lb 5 oz / 2 ¾ cups cream cheese
150 ml / 5 fl. oz / ⅔ cup soured cream
175 g / 6 oz / ¾ cup caster (superfine) sugar
2 large eggs, plus 1 egg yolk
2 tbsp plain (all-purpose) flour
1 tsp vanilla extract

For the topping:

100 g / 3 ½ oz / ⅓ cup redcurrant jelly
150 g / 5 ½ oz / 1 cup redcurrants

METHOD

- Preheat the oven to 180°C (160°C fan) / 350F / gas 4 and grease a 23 cm (9 in) round spring-form cake tin.

- Mix the biscuit crumbs with the butter and press into an even layer in the bottom of the tin. Bake the biscuit layer for 5 minutes or until firm.

- Whisk together the remaining ingredients until smooth. Spoon the cheesecake mixture on top of the biscuit base and bake for 50 minutes or until the centre is only just set. Leave to cool completely in the tin.

- To make the topping, heat the jelly in a small saucepan until runny then stir in the redcurrants and spoon on top of the cheesecake.

- Transfer the tin to the fridge and chill for 2 hours before unmoulding and cutting into slices.

CHOCOLATE FONDANTS

Makes: 6   Preparation time: 40 minutes   Cooking time: 8 minutes

INGREDIENTS
2 tbsp unsweetened cocoa powder
150 g / 5 ½ oz / 1 cup dark chocolate, minimum
    60% cocoa solids, chopped
150 g / 5 ½ oz / ⅔ cup butter, cubed
85 g / 3 oz / ⅓ cup caster (superfine) sugar
3 large eggs, plus 3 egg yolks
1 tbsp plain (all-purpose) flour

METHOD
- Oil 6 ring moulds and dust the insides with cocoa, then arrange them in a baking tin.
- Melt the chocolate, butter and sugar together in a saucepan, stirring to dissolve the sugar. Leave to cool a little then beat in the eggs and egg yolks and fold in the flour.
- Divide the mixture between the moulds, then chill for 30 minutes.
- Preheat the oven to 180°C (160°C fan) / 350F / gas 4.
- Bake the fondants for 8 minutes, then leave to cool for 2 minutes before unmoulding and serving.

BEER
THE
PUB
BEOIR
BIER
BIER

PROFITEROLES

Serves: 6   Preparation time: 1 hour   Cooking time: 20 minutes

INGREDIENTS

55 g / 2 oz / ¼ cup butter, cubed
75 g / 2 ½ oz / ½ cup strong white bread
    flour, sieved
2 large eggs, beaten
2 tbsp sugar nibs
225 ml / 8 fl. oz / 1 cup double (heavy) cream
100 g / 3 ½ oz / 1 cup icing (confectioners') sugar
1 tsp vanilla bean paste

For the chocolate sauce:

100 ml / 3 ½ fl. oz / ½ cup double (heavy) cream
1 tbsp brandy
100 g / 3 ½ oz / ½ cup dark chocolate (minimum
    60 % cocoa solids), chopped

METHOD

- Preheat the oven to 200°C (180°C fan) / 400F / gas 6. Line a baking tray with greaseproof paper and spray with a little water.

- Melt the butter with 150 ml / 5 fl. oz / ⅔ cup water and bring to the boil. Immediately beat in the flour, off the heat, with a wooden spoon until it forms a smooth ball of pastry. Incorporate the egg a little at a time to make a glossy paste.

- Spoon the pastry into a piping bag fitted with a large plain nozzle and pipe 2.5 cm (1 in) buns onto the baking tray. Sprinkle with sugar nibs.

- Bake for 20 minutes, increasing the temperature to 220°C (200°C fan) / 425F / gas 7 halfway through. Transfer the choux buns to a wire rack and make a hole in the underneath of each one so the steam can escape. Leave to cool completely.

- Whip the cream with the icing sugar and vanilla bean paste until it holds its shape, then spoon it into a piping bag. Fill the profiteroles with cream through the steam holes.

- To make the chocolate sauce, heat the cream and brandy to simmering point then pour it over the chocolate and stir to emulsify. Serve the profiteroles immediately with the hot chocolate sauce spooned over the top.

RASPBERRY RIPPLE ICE-CREAM

Serves: 6   Preparation time: 45 minutes   Cooking time: 10 minutes   Freezing time: 30 minutes

INGREDIENTS

450 ml / 12 ½ fl. oz / 1 ¾ cups whole milk
1 vanilla pod, split lengthways
4 large egg yolks
75 g / 2 ½ oz / ⅓ cup caster (superfine) sugar
200 g / 7 oz / 1 ⅓ cups raspberries
2 tbsp icing (confectioners') sugar
2 tbsp crème de framboise liqueur

METHOD

- Combine the milk and vanilla pod in a saucepan and bring to simmering point, then turn off the heat and leave to infuse for 20 minutes. Remove the vanilla pod.

- Whisk the egg yolks with the caster sugar until thick. Gradually incorporate the warm milk, whisking all the time, then scrape the mixture back into the saucepan.

- Stir the custard over a low heat until it just starts to thicken, then put the base of the pan in cold water and continue to stir until the custard cools a little and the danger of curdling has passed. Leave to cool to room temperature, then chill in the fridge.

- Press the raspberries through a sieve to remove the seeds, then stir in the icing sugar and framboise.

- Churn the custard in an ice-cream maker, according to the manufacturer's instructions. Fold through the raspberry sauce until nicely rippled, then spoon into a freezer container and freeze for 30 minutes to firm up.

- Scoop into sundae glasses and serve immediately.

CRÉME BRÛLÉE

Serves: 4   Preparation time: 45 minutes   Cooking time: 10 minutes

INGREDIENTS

450 ml / 12 ½ fl. oz / 1 ¾ cups whole milk
4 large egg yolks
75 g / 2 ½ oz / ⅓ cup caster (superfine) sugar
2 tsp cornflour (cornstarch)
1 tsp vanilla extract
4 tsp granulated sugar

METHOD

- Pour the milk into a saucepan and bring to simmering point.
- Meanwhile, whisk the egg yolks with the caster sugar, cornflour and vanilla extract until thick.
- Gradually incorporate the hot milk, whisking all the time, then scrape the mixture back into the saucepan.
- Stir the custard over a low heat until it thickens then divide it between 4 ramekins. Chill in the fridge for 25 minutes.
- Sprinkle the tops with granulated sugar then caramelise with a blow torch or under a hot grill.

INDEX

INDEX